Title: "Trail of Controversy: The Rise and Fall of Marjorie Taylor Greene"

Introduction:

Marjorie Taylor Greene's political career has been characterized by a series of controversial statements and actions that have drawn both national attention and criticism. Elected to the U.S. House of Representatives in 2020, she quickly became a polarizing figure due to her espousal of conspiracy theories, particularly the QAnon conspiracy, and her promotion of unfounded claims related to the 2020 presidential election.

Greene's background in business includes ownership of a construction company and a CrossFit gym. However, it is her political persona that has thrust her into the spotlight. Her views and statements have ranged from questioning the legitimacy of school shootings to expressing support for baseless claims about 9/11. Such positions have led to calls for her resignation and removal from congressional committees.

Despite facing censure from some members of her own party, Marjorie Taylor Greene has maintained a significant following among conservative and far-right circles. Her unwavering support for former President Donald Trump and her alignment with populist, anti-establishment sentiments have contributed to her staying power within the political landscape.

As a representative for Georgia's 14th congressional district, Greene continues to be a lightning rod for controversy, navigating the delicate balance between maintaining her loyal base and engaging with the broader responsibilities of legislative office. In the complex and evolving narrative of American politics, Marjorie Taylor Greene's presence remains a divisive force, emblematic of the challenges posed by extreme ideologies within the nation's democratic institutions.

Chapter 1: Roots of Radicalism

Marjorie Taylor Greene's journey into the world of far-right ideologies can be traced back to her formative years in Milledgeville, Georgia. Born to Robert Taylor, her early life set the stage for the controversial beliefs and extreme positions she would later embrace. Graduating from South Forsyth High School in Cumming, Georgia, in 1992, Greene then pursued higher education, obtaining a Bachelor of Business Administration from the University of Georgia in 1996.

However, a crucial event during her high school years left an indelible mark on Greene and played a pivotal role in shaping her views on gun rights and school shootings. In September 1990, she experienced a harrowing incident that would influence her perspective for years to come. The details of this event, which Greene later revealed, shed light on the roots of her staunch advocacy for gun rights and her controversial stance on issues related to school safety.

This chapter delves into Marjorie Taylor Greene's early life, exploring the environment in Milledgeville and the influences that contributed to the development of her far-right ideologies. The revelation of the impactful incident in 1990 serves as a key turning point, offering insights into the motivations behind Greene's later positions on firearms and her unyielding views on school shootings. By examining her roots, we gain a deeper understanding of the factors that set the stage for the controversial political figure she would become.

Chapter 2: Entrepreneurial Ventures and
Political Awakening

The evolution of Marjorie Taylor Greene's political identity intertwines with her foray into entrepreneurial ventures. In 2002, her father's sale of Taylor Commercial, a general-contracting company, marked a significant juncture. Taking the reins as vice president and president alongside her husband, Perry, the couple assumed leadership roles in the business. However, despite being formally listed as the chief financial officer from 2007 to 2011, investigations later raised questions about the extent of Greene's actual involvement in the company during that period.

Amidst her business endeavors, Greene's trajectory took an unexpected turn. In 2011, she relinquished her role as CFO and redirected her focus toward the fitness industry. Venturing into the world of CrossFit training, she co-founded CrossFit Passion in 2013. This chapter explores the dynamics of Greene's entrepreneurial ventures, scrutinizing her role in Taylor Commercial and the subsequent shift to the fitness sector.

Simultaneously, the narrative delves into the emergence of Marjorie Taylor Greene's political consciousness. The pivotal moment came during the 2016 Republican Party presidential primaries, a period that marked the beginning of her political awakening. As the chapter unfolds, it examines the factors and influences that propelled Greene from the business world into the realm of politics, setting the stage for her controversial entry onto the national stage.

Chapter 3: From Business to Conspiracy Theorist

The transition from the business world to the realm of conspiracy theories marked a significant chapter in Marjorie Taylor Greene's trajectory. By 2017, she had become a correspondent for the now-defunct American Truth Seekers, a conspiracy news website. This chapter delves into Greene's writings during this period, exploring the propagation of various extremist views. Her articles touched on government involvement in mass shootings, levied baseless allegations against the Clinton family, and delved into 9/11 conspiracy theories.

As she embraced the role of a conspiracy theorist, Greene's activities extended beyond online content creation. The narrative unfolds to explore her involvement with the Family America Project, an association marked by disturbing elements such as death threats against Democrats and explicit support for far-right ideologies. This phase of her journey solidified Marjorie Taylor Greene's reputation as a figure deeply entrenched in conspiracy theories, raising questions about the implications of her beliefs and the impact on her political ambitions.

Chapter 3 illuminates the pivotal moments and decisions that steered Greene from the business and fitness worlds into the controversial realm of conspiracy theories, setting the stage for the challenges and controversies that would later define her political career.

Chapter 4: Entry into Politics

Marjorie Taylor Greene's entry into the political arena unfolded against the backdrop of the 2020 United States House of Representatives elections in Georgia. This chapter traces the origins of her political aspirations, initially setting her sights on Georgia's 7th congressional district. However, a strategic shift in 2019 redirected her campaign to the 6th district. Later, with the retirement of Tom Graves, Greene pivoted once more, ultimately running for the 14th district.

The narrative explores the dynamics of Greene's campaign, characterized by unwavering support for Donald Trump, controversial endorsements, and a notable runoff election against neurosurgeon John Cowan. Her alignment with Trump's populist, anti-establishment sentiments endeared her to a significant base, while simultaneously drawing criticism for her controversial views and associations.

As the chapter unfolds, it examines the strategies, challenges, and controversies that defined Marjorie Taylor Greene's entry into electoral politics. From the initial district shuffle to the heated runoff election, her political journey underscores the complexities and divisions within the Republican Party during the 2020 elections and provides insights into the forces that propelled her to victory.

Chapter 5: Controversial Congressional Stint

Marjorie Taylor Greene's tenure as a U.S. representative has been marked by a series of controversies that have reverberated throughout the political landscape. This chapter delves into the controversies that have defined her congressional stint, beginning with her alignment with far-right conspiracy theories such as QAnon and Pizzagate. These affiliations culminated in her removal from all committee roles in February 2021, a significant setback that highlighted the challenges posed by her extreme beliefs within the halls of Congress.

Despite the committee removal, the narrative unfolds to reveal Greene's political resilience. By 2023, she managed to secure new committee roles, showcasing her ability to navigate the complex political terrain. However, her expulsion from the House Freedom Caucus in June 2023 serves as a poignant moment, underscoring the divisive nature of her presence in Congress. This chapter explores the dynamics surrounding her removal, the subsequent efforts to rebuild her political standing, and the ongoing tensions within the Republican Party that have been exacerbated by her controversial positions.

As Marjorie Taylor Greene navigates the complexities of her congressional role, the controversies surrounding her shed light on the broader challenges facing the political landscape and the ongoing debate over the boundaries of acceptable behavior within the United States Congress.

Chapter 6: A Controversial Victory

Marjorie Taylor Greene's journey to Congress climaxed in a highly contentious Republican runoff election against John Cowan. The chapter unfolds against the backdrop of a pivotal debate on July 14, where Cowan confronted Greene regarding Taylor Commercial's acceptance of Paycheck Protection Program (PPP) funds. This debate brought to light a seeming contradiction: while Greene vocally opposed congressional relief funds, her family-owned business had received $182,300 in PPP funding during the COVID-19 pandemic, ostensibly to preserve 12 jobs.

The narrative delves into the controversy surrounding Greene's financial dealings, particularly the subsequent revelation that approximately two months after receiving the PPP loan, she redirected $450,000 from her company to fund her political campaign. Despite these revelations and the ensuing public scrutiny, Marjorie Taylor Greene emerged victorious in the August 11 runoff, securing 57.1% of the votes.

The aftermath of her victory is marked by an endorsement from former President Donald Trump, who predicted Greene's ascent as a Republican star. This chapter examines the complex dynamics of the runoff election, the controversies surrounding Greene's financial decisions, and the political implications of her triumph within the broader context of Republican politics. It sheds light on the intricate interplay between personal finances, political campaigns, and the tumultuous journey that propelled Marjorie Taylor Greene into the national political spotlight.

Chapter 7: Unopposed Triumph

Following the Republican runoff, Marjorie Taylor Greene's path led to the general election for Georgia's 14th congressional district, historically a Republican stronghold. Positioned as the overwhelming favorite, Greene faced minimal opposition in a campaign that reflected the controversial nature that had come to define her political presence.

This chapter explores the dynamics of the general election, highlighting Greene's unopposed status in the traditionally Republican district. The narrative unfolds against the backdrop of a campaign marked by provocative tactics, including a controversial meme posted on Facebook. The meme featured Greene brandishing an AR-15 style rifle next to images of prominent Democrats, including Alexandria Ocasio-Cortez, Ilhan Omar, and Rashida Tlaib. The provocative imagery drew criticism, with House Speaker Nancy Pelosi characterizing it as a threat of violence.

Despite the controversies surrounding her campaign, Marjorie Taylor Greene secured a resounding victory in the general election, garnering 74.7% of the votes. Her triumph over Democratic candidate Kevin Van Ausdal, who had withdrawn from the race in September 2020, solidified her position as the representative for Georgia's 14th congressional district. This chapter explores the implications of Greene's unopposed triumph, the controversies that shadowed her path, and the resonance of her provocative campaign tactics within the broader political landscape

Chapter 8: The Early Days in Congress

Marjorie Taylor Greene's entry into Congress was marked by a series of bold and controversial actions, setting the tone for her early days in office. This chapter explores the events that unfolded as she stepped onto the national stage.

Upon assuming her congressional duties, Greene immediately attracted attention by wearing a face mask on her first day that boldly proclaimed "Trump Won," aligning herself with the baseless narrative of a stolen election. This overt display of allegiance foreshadowed her penchant for provocative gestures.

As Congress convened to count the electoral votes, Greene made headlines once again by objecting to the counting of Michigan's electoral votes, aligning herself with those challenging the legitimacy of the 2020 election results. This move, however, was ultimately rejected.

The narrative then delves into the aftermath of the January 6 United States Capitol attack. While calling for an end to violence, Greene's refusal to wear a face mask during the shelter-in-place period added another layer of controversy. Moreover, her response to the impeachment proceedings against then-President Donald Trump showcased a combative approach, deflecting blame onto Democrats.

Chapter 8 sheds light on the early days of Marjorie Taylor Greene's congressional tenure, examining the controversies and headline-grabbing moments that defined her initial presence in the legislative arena. The events during this period provide insight into her confrontational style and the impact of her actions on the broader political discourse.

Chapter 9: Expulsion and Political Maneuvers

As Marjorie Taylor Greene's tenure in Congress unfolded, the controversies surrounding her statements and affiliations intensified, triggering calls for expulsion and censure from her fellow lawmakers. Representative Jimmy Gomez took the lead by drafting a resolution aimed at expelling her from the House. Despite facing these challenges, Greene remained defiant, maintaining her controversial positions. Speaker Pelosi, acknowledging the heightened security concerns, underscored the presence of members like Greene who advocated bringing guns onto the House floor.

The narrative delves into a pivotal moment in June 2023 when Greene's expulsion from the Freedom Caucus transpired. This development followed a heated exchange with Congresswoman Lauren Boebert, exposing internal divisions within the caucus. The chapter explores the implications of Greene's removal from the caucus and the broader context of discord within Republican ranks.

Despite the setback, Greene continued to navigate the political landscape. The narrative unfolds to reveal her strategic maneuvers, including the introduction of resolutions aimed at expunging both of Donald Trump's impeachments. Notably, she gained support from House Minority Leader Kevin McCarthy, showcasing her ability to maintain political relevance despite facing internal and external challenges.

Chapter 9 examines the escalating tensions surrounding Marjorie Taylor Greene's congressional career, the internal divisions within the Republican Party, and her adept political maneuvers in the face of adversity. The events during this period illuminate the complex dynamics at play within Congress and the broader political landscape.

Chapter 10: Political Positions and Polarizing Rhetoric

Marjorie Taylor Greene's political journey has been defined by unwavering support for Donald Trump and a determined effort to shift the Republican Party further to the right. This chapter explores the specific political positions that have characterized her tenure in Congress.

With memberships in key caucuses such as the Election Integrity Caucus and the Second Amendment Caucus, Greene has positioned herself as a staunch advocate for conservative ideologies. Her commitment to these caucuses reflects a broader alignment with issues such as election integrity and gun rights that resonate strongly within conservative circles.

The narrative delves into Greene's positions on social issues, highlighting her staunch opposition to abortion and Planned Parenthood. False claims about contraceptive methods further underscore her conservative values, providing insight into the policy landscape she actively shapes.

Beyond her policy stances, the chapter explores the controversial rhetoric that has made Marjorie Taylor Greene one of the most polarizing figures in contemporary American politics. Her statements, both in person and on social media, have drawn widespread criticism from colleagues and the media, contributing to the divisive nature of her political presence.

Chapter 10 provides a comprehensive exploration of Marjorie Taylor Greene's political positions, shedding light on the ideological underpinnings that guide her legislative decisions and the polarizing rhetoric that has made her a central figure in the ongoing debates within the Republican Party and American politics at large.

Political Violence and Extremism (Continued):

The New York Times detailed Greene's support for and past ties with extremist militia groups, including the Three Percenters and the Oath Keepers. Both of these groups had members participate in the January 6, 2021, attack on the U.S. Capitol.

In an interview with gun activist Chris Dorr on October 27, 2020, just a week before the election, Greene told viewers: "the only way you get your freedoms back is it's earned with the price of blood."

Secession:

In late 2021, Greene advocated for a "national divorce" between red states and blue states. She suggested that red states disenfranchise people who move there from blue states for a period of five years. She repeated these suggestions in February 2023, facing condemnation from Democrats and some Republicans, including Spencer Cox, Liz Cheney, and Mitt Romney. The following day, Greene elaborated that she wants "a legal agreement" that would separate states more than they are now "while maintaining our legal union."

Evolution:

Greene has stated that she does not accept the scientific fact of evolution, calling it a "type of so-called science" and asserting, "I don't believe in evolution. I believe in God."

Climate Change:
Greene rejects the scientific consensus that climate change is caused primarily by human activity. She has expressed skepticism about climate change, suggesting that Earth's natural processes, rather than human actions, are responsible for climate fluctuations. She tweeted on April 15, 2023, calling climate change a "scam" and stating that "fossil fuels are natural and amazing." In the tweet, she included a chart that omitted carbon dioxide and methane, two major greenhouse gases.

LGBT Rights (Continued):
On August 19, 2022, Greene introduced the "Protect Children's Innocence Act," a bill that would make giving transgender youth gender-affirming care a felony punishable by up to 25 years in prison. The bill also seeks to prohibit the use of federal funds for gender-affirming care or health insurance covering it and prevent institutions of higher education from providing instruction on such care. Fourteen Republicans have co-sponsored the bill. In November 2022, after California state senator Scott Wiener, who is gay, criticized the use of the term "groomer" as an anti-LGBTQ hate word, Greene responded that the Protect Children's Innocence Act would stop "communist groomers" such as Wiener.

Race, Religion, and Immigration (Continued):
Greene opposes the Black Lives Matter movement, describing it as a Marxist group. In a video, she compared Black Lives Matter activists to white nationalist participants at the August 2017 Unite the Right rally in Charlottesville, Virginia. She has claimed that the most mistreated group in the United States today is white males. After the murder of George Floyd, Greene posted on Facebook that his death "must be investigated and justice will be served," calling the video "heartbreaking." However, when Derek Chauvin was found guilty of Floyd's murder, Greene claimed the verdict resulted from jury intimidation by Black Lives Matter and falsely asserted that Washington, D.C. was "completely dead" on the night of the verdict due to people being "scared to go out" for "fear of riots."

In a recording obtained by Politico, Greene said that Muslims who believe in Sharia law should not be in the U.S. government. She also contended that the Democratic Party is holding Black Americans as "slaves." Her comments on black people, Muslims, and Jews were denounced by Republican House leaders and a spokesman for National Republican Congressional Committee chairman Tom Emmer. Greene said that the election of Ilhan Omar and Rashida Tlaib in the 2018 midterm elections was part of "an Islamic invasion of our government."

Secession:

In late 2021, Greene advocated for a "national divorce" between red states and blue states. She suggested that red states disenfranchise people who move there from blue states for a period of five years. She repeated these suggestions in February 2023, facing condemnation from Democrats and some Republicans, including Spencer Cox, Liz Cheney, and Mitt Romney. The following day, Greene elaborated that she wants "a legal agreement" that would separate states more than they are now "while maintaining our legal union."

Political Violence and Extremism (Continued):

In an interview with gun activist Chris Dorr on October 27, 2020, just a week before the election, Greene told viewers: "the only way you get your freedoms back is it's earned with the price of blood." On January 29, 2021, The New York Times detailed Greene's support for and past ties with extremist militia groups, including the Three Percenters and the Oath Keepers. Both of these groups had members participate in the January 6, 2021, attack on the U.S. Capitol.

This covers additional information on Marjorie Taylor Greene's positions and actions on various issues. If you have further questions or need more details, feel free to ask.

Rhetoric Involving Killing of Opponents:
Marjorie Taylor Greene has faced significant controversy for her rhetoric involving the killing of opponents. In a January 2019 Facebook video, she accused Nancy Pelosi of treason, claiming it was a crime punishable by death. Greene promoted a petition to impeach Pelosi for treason, despite the fact that such a remedy does not exist in the U.S. Constitution. In February 2019, she visited Pelosi's office and suggested that Pelosi would either be killed or imprisoned for treason. Greene also made similar claims about Representative Maxine Waters.

Additionally, in 2018 and 2019, Greene's Facebook account expressed support for the execution of leading Democrats, including Pelosi, Barack Obama, and Hillary Clinton, as well as FBI agents. She did not deny the authenticity of these posts but claimed they were from a time before she ran for political office.

Advocacy Based on Conspiracy Theories:
Marjorie Taylor Greene has been a vocal proponent of various conspiracy theories, raising concerns and condemnation from both Democrats and Republicans. Some of the conspiracy theories she has promoted include:

Claiming that Hillary Clinton is responsible for a series of murders.
Alleging that Democratic Party elites are involved in a satanic child sex trafficking ring.
Suggesting that the government orchestrated the 2017 Las Vegas shooting.
Claiming that the Stoneman Douglas High School shooting in Parkland, Florida, was a false flag attack intended to promote gun control.
Propagating the false idea that the Sandy Hook Elementary School shooting was staged.
Alleging that Barack Obama secretly visited North Korea and sabotaged nuclear diplomacy.
Spreading the false claim that Obama and his advisor Valerie Jarrett were secretly Muslim.
Propagating the idea that the September 11 attack on the Pentagon was fake.
Promoting the conspiracy theory that the U.S. government is planning to force Americans to eat fake meat grown by Bill Gates.
Greene's promotion of these conspiracy theories has drawn criticism for spreading disinformation and contributing to a climate of mistrust.

Pizzagate and QAnon:
Marjorie Taylor Greene has expressed belief in the debunked Pizzagate conspiracy theory, claiming links between Hillary Clinton and pedophilia and human sacrifice. She has also supported the QAnon conspiracy theory, claiming that there is a global cabal of Satan-worshipping pedophiles that needs to be taken down.

It's important to note that both Pizzagate and QAnon are baseless conspiracy theories that have been widely discredited.

False Flag Claims:
Greene has expressed doubt about various tragic events, suggesting they were false flag operations:

Doubting that the perpetrator of the 2017 Las Vegas shooting acted alone.
Claiming that the Charlottesville white nationalist rally in 2017 was an "inside job."
Suggesting that the 2019 Christchurch mosque shootings in New Zealand were a false flag operation.
Expressing support for the conspiracy theory that a plane did not hit the Pentagon during the September 11 attacks.
These claims have been widely criticized for spreading misinformation and undermining public trust in historical events.

Shootings:
Greene has made controversial statements regarding school shootings:

Claiming that the 2018 Stoneman Douglas High School shooting in Parkland, Florida, was an organized false flag operation.
Suggesting that the 2012 Sandy Hook Elementary School shooting was also a false flag operation.
Alleging that Nancy Pelosi told Hillary Clinton that "we need another school shooting" to persuade the public to support strict gun control.
These statements have faced strong condemnation, particularly from survivors of the Parkland shooting.

Georgia Guidestones Bombing:
Greene criticized the Georgia Guidestones and, in an interview with Alex Jones, suggested that ecumenical texts inscribed on the monument represented a nefarious future of "population control" envisioned by the "hard left." The Guidestones were later dynamited by unknown saboteurs.

Antisemitism and White Genocide Conspiracy Theory:
In 2018, Greene shared a video promoting the antisemitic white genocide conspiracy theory, suggesting that Zionists are conspiring to flood Europe with migrants to replace native white populations. She has also falsely called George Soros, a Jewish businessman and Holocaust survivor, a Nazi.

These instances of antisemitism and promotion of a baseless conspiracy theory have drawn condemnation from various organizations and individuals.

Removal from House Committee Assignments:
Due to the controversy surrounding Greene's statements and conspiracy theories, the House voted to remove her from committee assignments in February 2021. The vote was 230 to 199, with 11 Republicans joining all Democrats. Greene described herself as "freed" after the vote, criticizing the committees as part of a "tyrannically controlled government."

Marjorie Taylor Greene's controversial statements and promotion of conspiracy theories have sparked significant debate and criticism, both within and outside of Congress. If you have more specific questions or if there's anything else you'd like to know, feel free to ask.

Made in the USA
Las Vegas, NV
05 January 2024

83919773R00017